Published 2020 by Macmillan Children's Books
an imprint of Pan Macmillan
The Smithson, 6 Briset Street, London EC1M 5NR
Associated companies throughout the world
www.panmacmillan.com

ISBN 978-1-5290-4366-2

1 3 5 7 9 8 6 4 2

A CIP catalogue record for this book is available from the British Library.
Compiled and illustrated by Perfect Bound Ltd
Illustrated by Dan Newman and Grace Newman

Printed and bound by CPI Group (UK) Ltd, Croydon CR0 4YY

SPOOKY
JOKES

CONTENTS

TOMB IT MAY CONCERN

What's the difference between a deer running away and a small witch?

One's a hunted stag, the other's a stunted hag.

What is a baby ghost's favourite game?

Peeka-boo!

What is a vampire's favourite
ice-cream flavour?
Veinilla!

Why do witches fly on broomsticks?
**Vacuum-cleaner cords
aren't long enough.**

What fairy tale do ghosts like best?
Sleeping Boo-ty!

Why didn't the
skeleton cross
the road?
**He didn't have
the guts.**

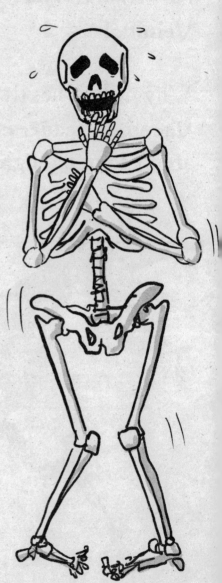

What type of
dog do vampires
like the best?
Bloodhounds!

Do zombies eat popcorn
with their fingers?
No, they eat the fingers separately.

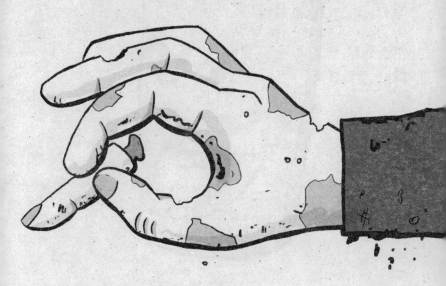

What kind of ghosts
haunt skyscrapers?
High spirits!

What's red, sweet and bites people?
A jampire!

Why do mummies have
trouble making friends?
**They're too wrapped
up in themselves.**

What happened when the little witch was naughty at school?
She was ex-spelled.

What's a monster's favourite bean?
A human bean.

How do ghosts like their eggs cooked?
Terrifried!

What do skeletons say before eating?
Bone appetit!

What goes cackle, cackle, boom?
A witch in a minefield.

'Mummy, Mummy, all the
kids call me a werewolf!'
**'Never mind, dear, now go
and comb your face.'**

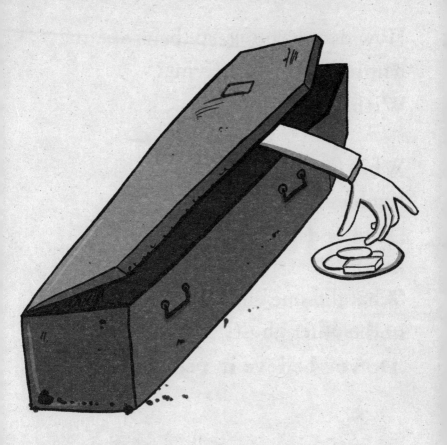

Why wasn't the vampire working?
He was on a coffin break.

What do you call a dead chicken
that likes to scare people?
A poultrygeist!

How do witches keep their
hair in place while flying?
With scare spray...

What kind of streets do
zombies like best?
Dead ends!

What did one ghost say
to the other ghost?
'Do you believe in people?'

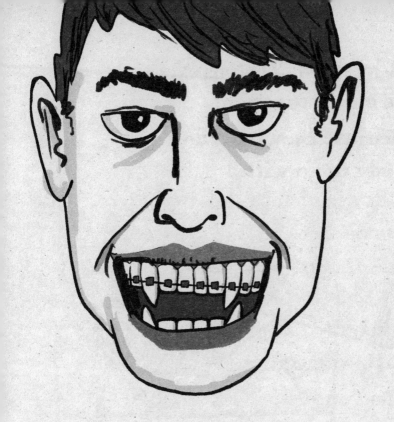

Why did the vampire go
to the orthodontist?
To improve his bite.

What does the ghost say
when it gets into the car?
'Fasten your sheet belts.'

Why don't skeletons ever
go out on the town?
**Because they have no
body to go with.**

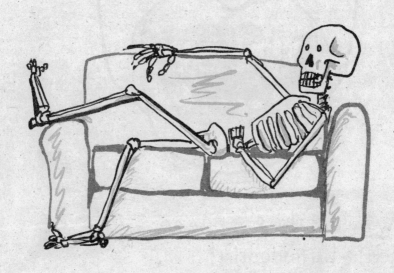

What is warty, evil and
goes round and round?
A witch in a revolving door!

How did the glamorous
ghoul earn her living?
She was a cover ghoul...

What do you get when you cross
a vampire and a snowman?
Frostbite!

What happens when a ghost
gets lost in the fog?

He is mist.

What do they teach at witch school?

Spelling!

What's big and green and
goes 'oink, oink'?
Frankenswine!

What did the skeleton say
to the bartender?
'I'll have two Cokes and a mop.'

What did Dracula say when his
vampire girlfriend kissed him?
'Ouch.'

What's a vampire's favourite dance?
The fangdango!

What do ghosts have for dessert?
Ice scream!

Why did the witch wash her broom?
She wanted a clean sweep.

DEAD RECKONING

Who was the famous
skeleton detective?
Sherlock Bones.

What do you call a lost monster?
A where-wolf!

Where did the vampire
keep his valuables?
In a blood bank!

Why don't mummies go on holidays?
**They're afraid they'll
relax and unwind.**

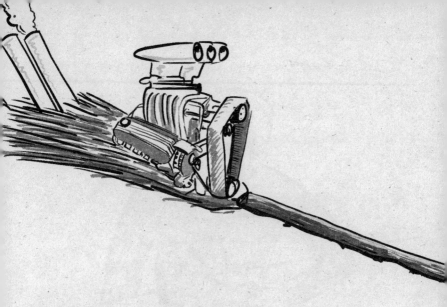

What do witches have races on?
Brrrrrrroomsticks!

What happened to the wolf who
fell into a washing machine?
He became a wash-and-werewolf.

What kind of spirits serve
food on a plane?
Air ghostesses!

What do young ghouls write
their homework in?
Exorcise books!

What is a skeleton's favourite
musical instrument?
A trombone!

How does a vampire flirt?
They bat their eyes.

Why didn't the witch wear a flat cap?
There was no point in it.

What does a skeleton
order at a restaurant?
Spare ribs!

What kind of ghost has
the best hearing?
The eeriest!

Where does Dracula have lunch?
At the casketeria...

How can you tell if a witch
is carrying a timebomb?
You can hear their brooms tick.

Who won the skeleton beauty contest?
No body.

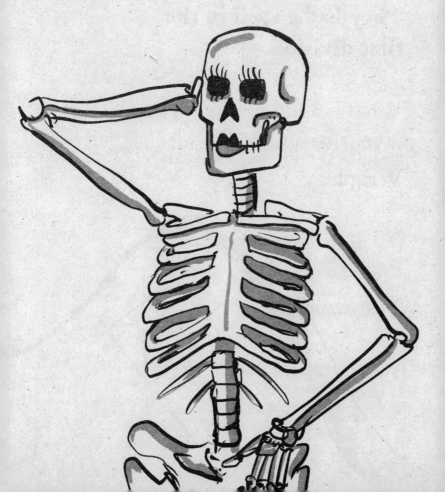

What did the mummy
say to the detective?
'Let's wrap this case up.'

How did the witches'
basketball team do?
**They had a spell in the
first division.**

What is a mummy's
favourite type of music?
Wrap!

Why doesn't anybody like Dracula?
He has a bat temper.

What ride do spirits like the
best at the amusement park?
The rollerghoster!

How do you join the Dracula fan club?
Send your name, address and blood group.

Why did the one-eyed monster have to close his school?
He only had one pupil.

What kind of pets do ghosts have?
Scaredy cats!

How did the vampire marathon go?
It finished neck and neck.

What kind of piano music
do witches play?
Hag-time!

How do you make a witch scratch?
Just take away the W.

Why do skeletons hate winter?
**Because the cold goes
right through them.**

Why shouldn't you grab a
werewolf by the tail?
**It might be the werewolf's tail,
but it could be the end of you!**

GRRRRRRR

Have you heard about the
good-weather witch?
She's forecasting sunny spells.

Why did the ghost starch her sheet?
So she could scare everyone stiff.

29

Why don't angry witches
ride their brooms?
**They're afraid of flying
off the handle.**

Why are skeletons so calm?
Nothing gets under their skin.

Why does Dracula take art classes?
He likes to draw blood.

Where do ghosts go on Saturday nights?
Anywhere they can boo-gie.

What was the cold, evil candle called?
The Wicked Wick of the North.

EM-BALMY ABOUT YOU

What does a ghost have on top
of his ice-cream sundae?

Whipped scream!

What do you get if you cross
Dracula with Sir Lancelot?
A bite in shining armour...

Why are so few ghosts arrested?
**It's impossible to pin
anything on them.**

What do you call a
monster with no neck?
The Lost Neck Monster!

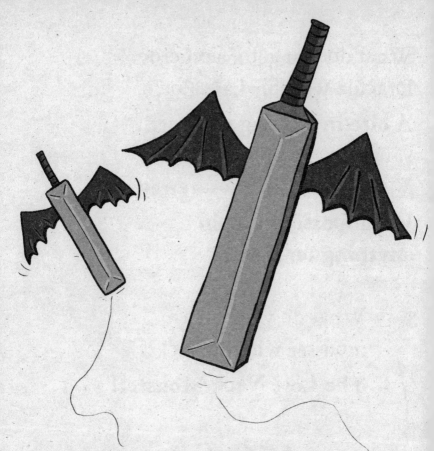

Why did the vampires cancel
their cricket game?

They couldn't find their bats.

Why did the skeleton jump
on a trampoline?

To have a rattling good time.

Ghost: Where do fleas go in winter?
Werewolf: Search me!

What has six legs and flies?
A witch giving her cat a lift.

How do you get milk
from a witch's cat?
Steal her saucer.

What did the baby vampire say
before going to bed?
**Turn on the dark –
I'm afraid of the light.**

What does a child monster
call his parents?
Mummy and Deady!

What kind of ghosts haunt
operating theatres?
Surgical spirits!

Why did the witch celebrate?
She passed her hex-animations.

What do you call a stupid skeleton?
Bonehead!

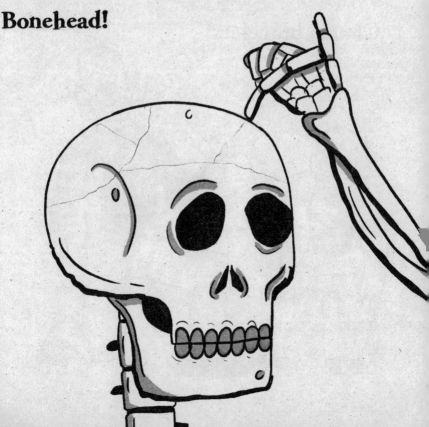

What is Dracula's favourite fruit?
A neck-tarine!

What game do ghosts play at parties?
Hide-and-shriek!

What kind of jewellery
do witches wear?
Charm bracelets!

Where do ghosts post their letters?
At the ghost office.

What do you do when fifty
zombies surround your house?
Hope it's Halloween...

Why do demons and ghouls
hang out together?

**Because demons are a
ghoul's best friend.**

What is as sharp as a vampire's fang?

His other fang...

Why are vampires like false teeth?

They come out at night.

What do you call a witch
who lives at the beach?
A sand-witch.

Why did the game warden
arrest the ghost?
He didn't have a haunting licence.

What do you get if you cross
a witch with an iceberg?
Cold spells!

What do you get if you cross
a dinosaur with a wizard?
Tyrannosaurus hex!

What do you call ghost children?
Boys and ghouls...

What do you call two witches
who live together?
Broommates!

Why did the skeleton stay
up late studying?
He was boning up for his exams.

Why are pixies such messy eaters?
**Because they are always
goblin their food.**

What is a ghost's favourite
means of transportation?
A scareplane!

Why did Dracula visit the doctor?
Because of his coffin...

Why do vampires need mouthwash?
They have bat breath.

How do you keep a monster
from biting his nails?
Give him some screws.

Why did the vampire subscribe
to the *Wall Street Journal*?
He heard it had great circulation.

What kind of make-up do ghouls wear?
Mas-scare-a!

What story do little witches
like to hear at bedtime?
Ghoul deluxe and the three scares!

BLOODBATH

Why did the headless
horseman go into business?
He wanted to get ahead in life.

Why do ghosts go on diets?
**So they can keep their
ghoulish figures.**

What is a ghoul's favourite drink?
Lemon and slime!

Where do fashionable
ghosts shop for sheets?
At boo-tiques!

What should you say when
you meet a ghost?
'How do you boo?'

Where does Dracula stay
when he's in New York?
At the Vampire State Building!

Why were ancient Egyptian
children confused?
**Because they couldn't tell their
daddies from their mummies.**

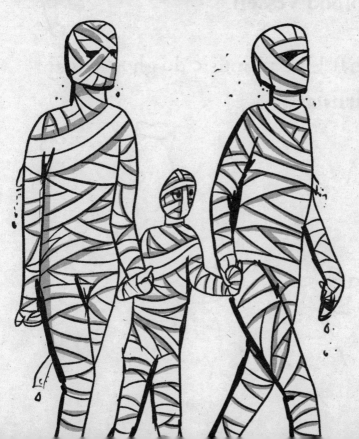

What do you get when you
cross a ghost with an owl?
**Something that scares people
and doesn't give a hoot.**

What is a vampire's favourite
means of transportation?
A blood vessel!

What kind of music do ghosts like?
Spirituals!

How can you tell if a
vampire likes cricket?
Every night he turns into a bat.

Who was the most famous
French skeleton?
Napoleon Bone-apart!

What do you call a wizard
from outer space?
A flying sorcerer.

What does a ghoul get when he
comes home late for dinner?
The cold shoulder!

Why isn't Dracula invited
to many parties?

He's a bit of a pain in the neck.

Why are ghosts like newspapers?

Because they appear in sheets.

How do monsters tell their future?
They read their horrorscope.

What did the plumber say when he
was called to the vampire's house?
It's a grave problem.

What's a ghost's favourite party game?
Musical Graves!

Who did the ghost invite to his party?
Anyone he could dig up.

What do wizards stop
for on motorways?
Witchhikers!

What happened when the
ghosts went on strike?
A skeleton staff took over.

What keeps ghouls happy?
**The knowledge that every
shroud has a silver lining!**

Who does Dracula get letters from?
His fang club!

What did the ghost teacher
say to her class?
**'Watch the board and I'll
go through it again!'**

What does Dracula
drink at breakfast?
**Coffin with
scream and sugar.**

What would you get if you
crossed a vampire with a snail?
**I don't know, but it would
slow him down.**

Why did the twin witches
wear name tags?
**So they could tell which
witch was which!**

What is a ghost's favourite holiday?
April Ghoul's Day!

What airline do ghouls fly with?
British Scareways!

What happened when the
ghost met the zombie?
It was love at first fright.

What do you call a prehistoric ghost?
A terror-dactyl!

What is Dracula's favourite
kind of coffee?
Decoffinated!

What do little ghosts
wear when it rains?
Boo-ts or ghoul-oshes!

What happened to the guy
who didn't pay his exorcist?
He was repossessed.

What kind of jewels do ghouls wear?
Tombstones!

ABSOLUTELY MONSTROUS!

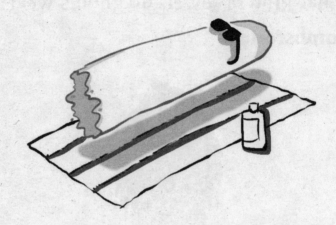

Where do ghosts go on holidays?
Mali-boo!

Why can't skeletons play
music in church?
Because they have no organs.

What do you give a vampire with a cold?
Coffin drops!

What goes 'ha, ha, ha' – thud?
**A monster laughing
his head off**

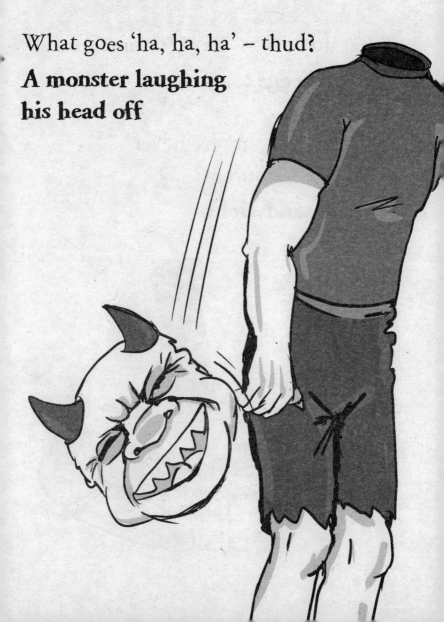

What trees do ghouls like best?
Ceme-trees!

What do demons have for breakfast?
Devilled eggs...

What does a vampire never
order at a restaurant?
A stake sandwich!

What do you call a dead cow
that's come back to life?
Zombeef!

How do ghosts begin a letter?
Tomb it may concern...

What happened to the ghost
who was a bad actor?

He was booed off the stage.

What goes around wailing,
wears a white sheet and always
points to the north?

A magnetic ghost...

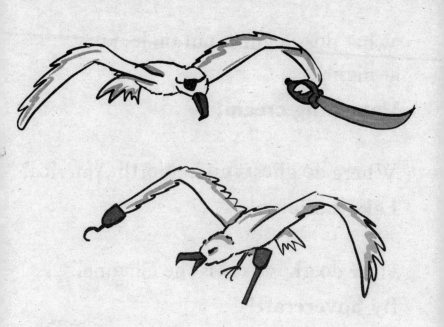

What do you get if you cross
a ghost with a sailor?
A sea-ghoul!

What do you call a phantom hen?
A poultry-geist!

Why did the ghost look in the mirror?
To see if he still wasn't there.

What does a ghost put on its face
at night?
Vanishing cream!

Where do ghosts go in North America?
Lake Eerie...

How do ghosts cross the Channel?
By hovercraft!

Where do ghosts like to swim?
The Dead Sea!

What screams more loudly than
a person frightened by a ghost?
Two people frightened by a ghost...

What do ghosts who've been in hospital enjoy?

Talking about their apparition...

What do you get if you cross a ghost with a packet of crisps?

Snacks that go crunch in the night!

What did the short-sighted ghost wear?

Spooktacles!

What did the jailer say to the ghost
of Charles I?
You must be off your head.

What would you do if a ghost
floated through your front door?
Run out of your back door!

Why couldn't the ghost stand up?
It had no visible means of support.

A ghost walked into a pub and
asked for a large whisky.

   **'Sorry,' said the barman, 'I'm
afraid we don't serve spirits.'**

How does a ghost pass
through a locked door?
He uses a skeleton key.

Knock, knock.
'Who's there?'
'Fred.'
'Fred who?'
'Are you Fred of ghosts?'

Why do ghosts
like tall buildings?
**They have
lots of
scarecases.**

Why do spooks like riding horses?
They like ghoulloping.

What is a ghost's favourite
day of the week?
Moanday!

How can you recognize
a ghost's bicycle?
By the spooks in its wheels...

What do you call a play
acted by ghosts?
A phantomime!

What is a ghost's favourite country?
Wails!

How do worried ghosts look?

Grave...

What kind of music does
a ghost enjoy?

A haunting melody!

What's a ghost's favourite
TV programme?

Horror-nation Street.

SPOOK WHEN YOU'RE SPOOKEN TO

What's it called when a ghost makes a mistake?

A boo-boo!

Why did the ghost go to hospital?
To have his ghoulstones removed.

What's an undertaker's
favourite town?
Gravesend!

What's an undertaker's motto?
The morgue the merrier.

How can you avoid dying?
Stay in the living room.

Why are there fences
around graveyards?
Because people are dying to get in.

What's the difference between a musician and a corpse?

One composes, the other decomposes.

Why can't you be lonely in a graveyard?

There's always some body there.

How can you recognize an undertaker?

By his grave manner...

Why is it difficult to bury an elephant?
Because it's a huge undertaking.

How can you tell if a
mummy is angry?
He flips his lid.

Why are mummies so good
at keeping secrets?
They keep everything under wraps.

What do mummies wear
on their fingernails?
Nile varnish!

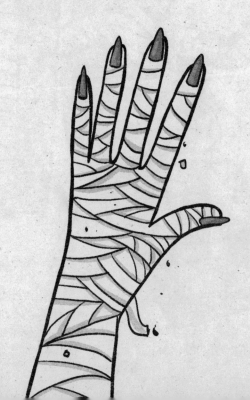

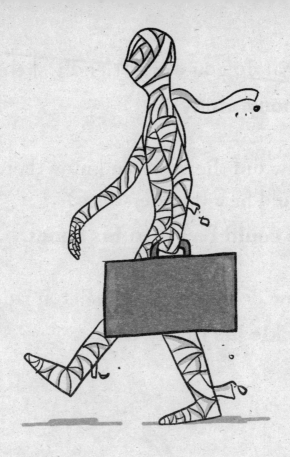

Why did the mummy leave his tomb?
**After 5,000 years, he thought he
was old enough to leave home.**

What do you call a mummy
who eats biscuits in bed?
A crumby mummy!

What do you call a friendly skeleton?
A bony crony!

How did the skeleton know there
would be a thunderstorm?
He could feel it in his bones.

How do you make a skeleton laugh?
Tickle his funny bone.

What do you get if you cross
a skeleton with a python?
A rattlesnake!

Why didn't the skeleton
leave his grave?
He didn't have the guts.

What did the skeleton say to his wife?
I love every bone in your body.

Why do skeleton's drink milk?
It's good for the bones.

What do you call a skeleton
that stays in bed all day?
Lazy bones!

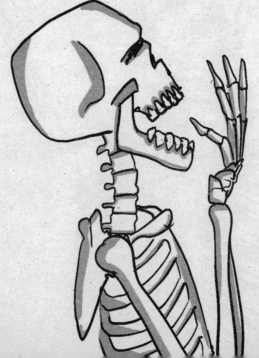

Who sailed the phantom ship?
A skeleton crew!

Why was the skeleton
no good at his job?
His heart wasn't in it.

What do skeletons sell at fêtes?
Rattle tickets!

Why did Dracula employ
young vampires?
He liked new blood in the business.

What do you call a short vampire?
A pain in the leg...

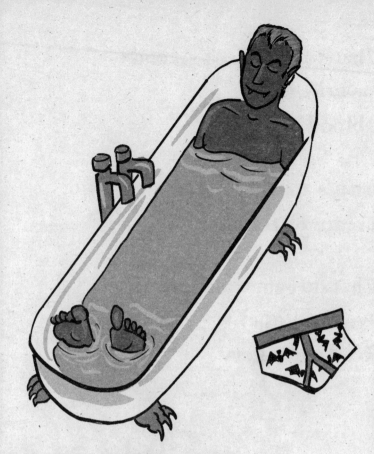

What do vampires take
before going to bed?
A bloodbath!

What wears a black cape, flies
around at night and sucks blood?
A mosquito in a black cape...

What's a vampire's second-favourite fruit?

A blood orange!

What's a zombie's favourite soup?

Scream of tomato!

What do baby vampires say at bedtime?

'Read me a gory.'

What do vampires like for breakfast?
Ready neck!

Why is it easy to trick vampires?
Because they're all suckers...

WHO'S FOR DINNER?

What's a vampire's favourite pudding?
Leeches and scream!

How does Dracula keep fit?
He plays batminton.

Why did the vampire carry his coffin around with him?
Because his life was at stake.

What happened when
the boy vampire met the
girl vampire?
It was love at first bite.

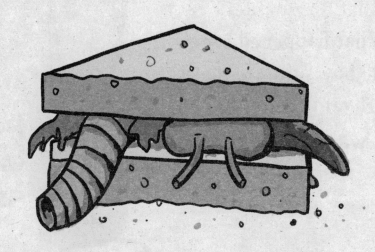

What do vampires eat with
bread and cheese?
Pickled organs!

What does a polite vampire say?
'Fangs a lot.'

Why did the vampire and
the ghost hang out?
They were the best of fiends.

What do zombies like to
read every week?
Their horror-scopes!

What does a vampire call
a new set of dentures?
A new-fangled device!

Why do vampires eat mints?
Because they often have bat breath.

Why didn't Dracula want
to get married?
He enjoyed the bat-chelor life.

What's pink, has a curly
tail and drinks blood?
A hampire!

Why was Dracula sad?
He loved in vein.

Dracula was in a boxing match where he knocked his opponent out.
He was Out for the Count.

Where do vampires live?
In a far-off terror-tory...

Why do vampires and
piranhas get along?
They're both fang-tastic.

How does Frankenstein eat his dinner?
He bolts it down.

What did Frankenstein say when
he was struck by lightning?
'Phew, I needed that.'

What did the sea monster say
when it saw a submarine?
'Oh good, more tinned food.'

What's a monster's favourite ballet?
Swamp Lake...

How do monsters count
up to a hundred?
On their fingers...

How do monster snowmen
feel when they melt?
Abominable!

Who has feathers, fangs and quacks?
Count Duckula!

What did the monster eat after the
dentist took out all his teeth?
The dentist...

What do you call a vampire rooster?
Count Cluckula!

How do zombies like
their shepherd's pie?
Made with real shepherds...

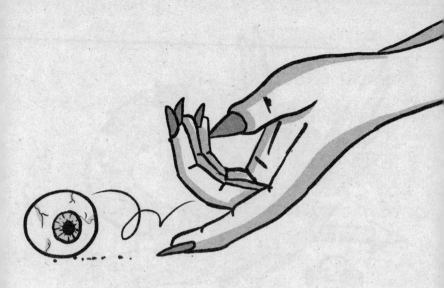

What should you do when a
monster rolls their eyes at you?
Roll them back!

Which ghost was the
president of France?
Charles de Ghoul!

Why do dragons sleep during the day?
So they can fight knights.

Why was the zombie tired?
He felt dead on his feet.

What monster lives in your nose?
A bogeyman!

Why does Frankenstein
have good posture?
He always sits bolt upright.

Why is Frankenstein fun to be with?
He'll always have you in stitches.

Who does a zombie take to the cinema?
Any old friend he can dig up...

What do teachers say to
young ghosts at school?
**'Only spook when
you're spooken to.'**

What do sea monsters like for supper?
Fish and ships!

THAT'S THE SPIRIT!

What do ghosts eat for breakfast?
Dreaded wheat!

Why did the monster get
good marks in the exam?
**Because two heads are
better than one...**

How does a ghost count to ten?
One, boo, three, four, five, six, seven, hate, nine, frighten!

Which ghost works in parliament?
The Spooker of the House of Commons...

Who writes a spook's biography?
A ghost writer!

Why did the man marry a ghost?
He didn't know what possessed him.

Who keeps watch for scary ships?
The ghost guard!

Where do ghouls go on their holidays?
The Ghosta Brava!

Where do baby ghosts go during
the day?
Day-scare centre...

How do ghosts keep fit?

By regular exorcise...

What would you find in the cellar of a haunted house?

Whines and spirits...

What do ghosts like to chew?
BOO-bble gum!

Knock, knock.
'Who's there?'
'Spectre.'
'Spectre who?'
'Spectre of police, you're under arrest.'

Why do ghosts love going on holiday?
They always have a wail of a time.

What do you call a ghost shepherdess?
Little Boo Peep!

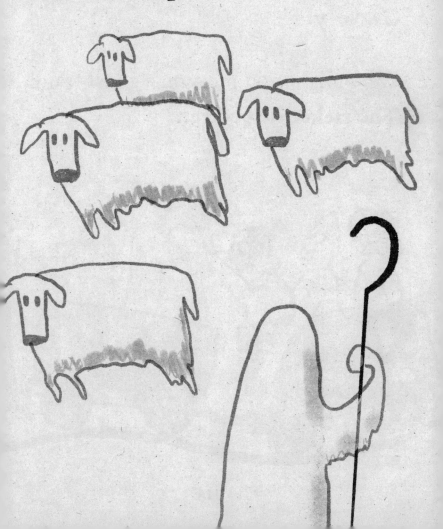

What walks through a wall
and goes 'oooooob'?
A ghost walking backwards.

What do zombies eat with roast beef?
Grave-y!

Who might you meet on a ghost train?
The ticket inspectre...

Did you hear about the man
who didn't know the meaning
of the word 'fear'?

He was too scared to ask.

How does a spook travel
around the world?

She goes from ghost to ghost.

What do you call a ghost
that haunts a hospital?
A surgical spirit!

Why did the headless horseman
take a bag of oats to bed with him?
To feed his nightmares...

What is a ghost's favourite
Italian dish?
Spookhetti!

Who's the most important player
in a ghost football team?
The ghoul-keeper!

What's a gargoyle?
**Something a monster does
when it has a sore throat...**

How did the ghost travel to America?
**It took off from Heathrow
on a night fright.**

What shoes do ghosts wear in winter?
Boooooooots!

Where do ghosts wash their clothes?
The dry-screamers!

Why did the zombie do so well
in his exam?

Because it was a no-brainer...

Why did everyone laugh at the ghost?

He kept making a ghoul of himself.

What do zombies eat for tea?
Baked beings on toast...

What do you serve a witch's tea in?
A cup and a sorcerer!

Why couldn't the young
witch write a letter?
She hadn't learned to spell.

Two members of the circus were talking about a former colleague who worked as a magician, and his trick was sawing people in half.

'An odd fellow,' remarked a clown. 'Was he an only child?'

'Oh, no', replied the elephant trainer. 'I believe he had lots of half-brothers and sisters.'

Noisy Ghouls and Werewolves
Mona Lott

When Zombies Attack!
Claudia Armoff

Undertaker Tales
Paul Bearer

Ghosts Aren't Real
Madge Innery

How to Re-animate a Monster
Alec Tricity & Jenny Rater

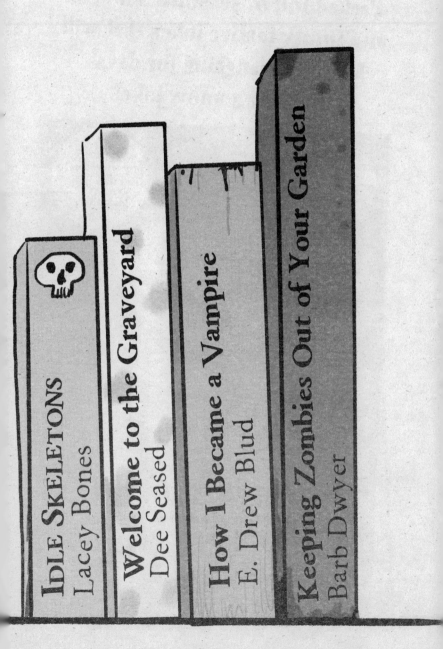

IDLE SKELETONS
Lacey Bones

Welcome to the Graveyard
Dee Seased

How I Became a Vampire
E. Drew Blud

Keeping Zombies Out of Your Garden
Barb Dwyer

Packed full of seasonal silliness
and funny festive jokes that will
keep you laughing for days –
and that's snow joke!